THE PINTEREST TATTOO COOKBOOK

DEVIN SHEEHY

PORKOPOLIS PRODUCTIONS
CINCINNATI, OH

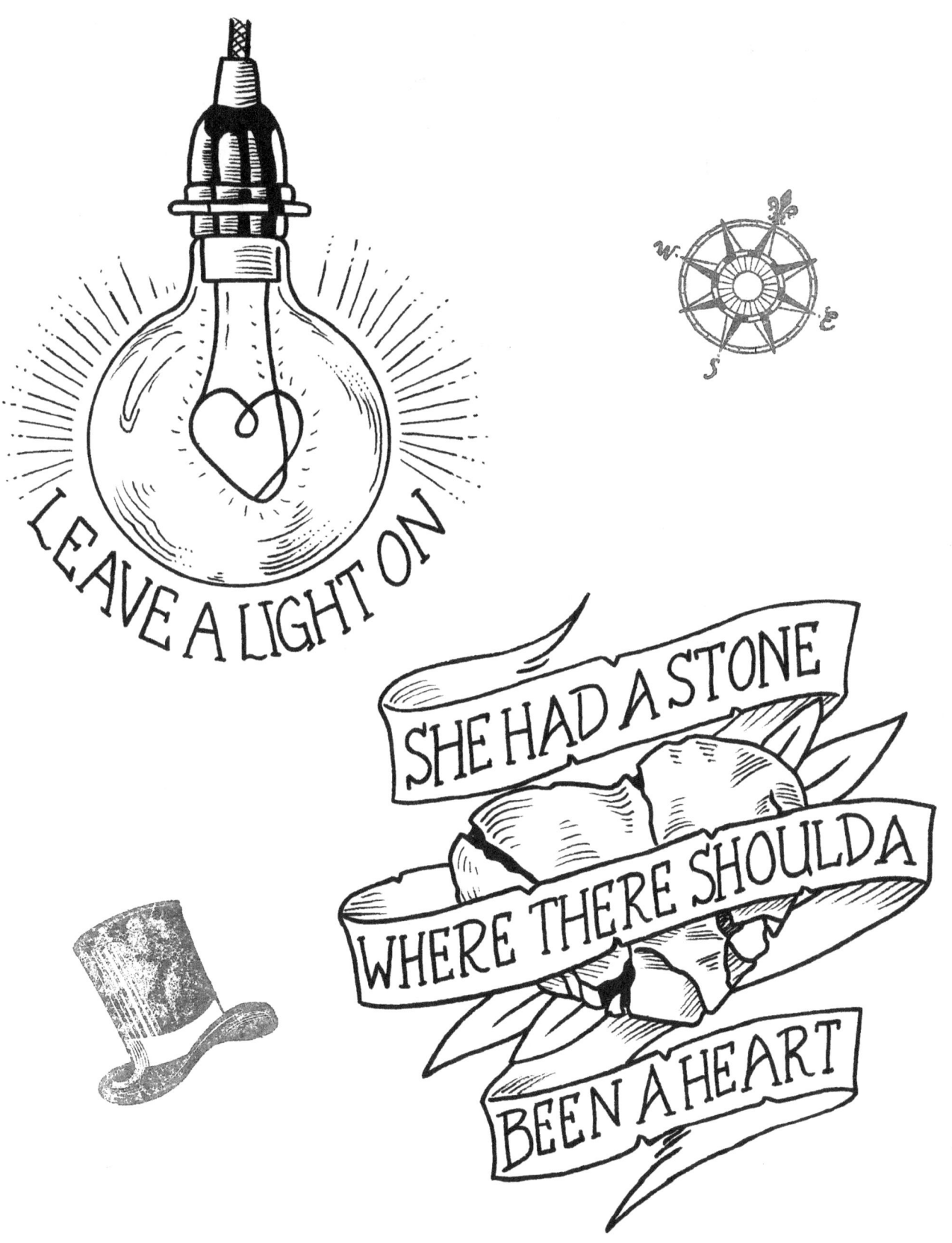

LEAVE A LIGHT ON

SHE HAD A STONE WHERE THERE SHOULDA BEEN A HEART

Devin Sheehy

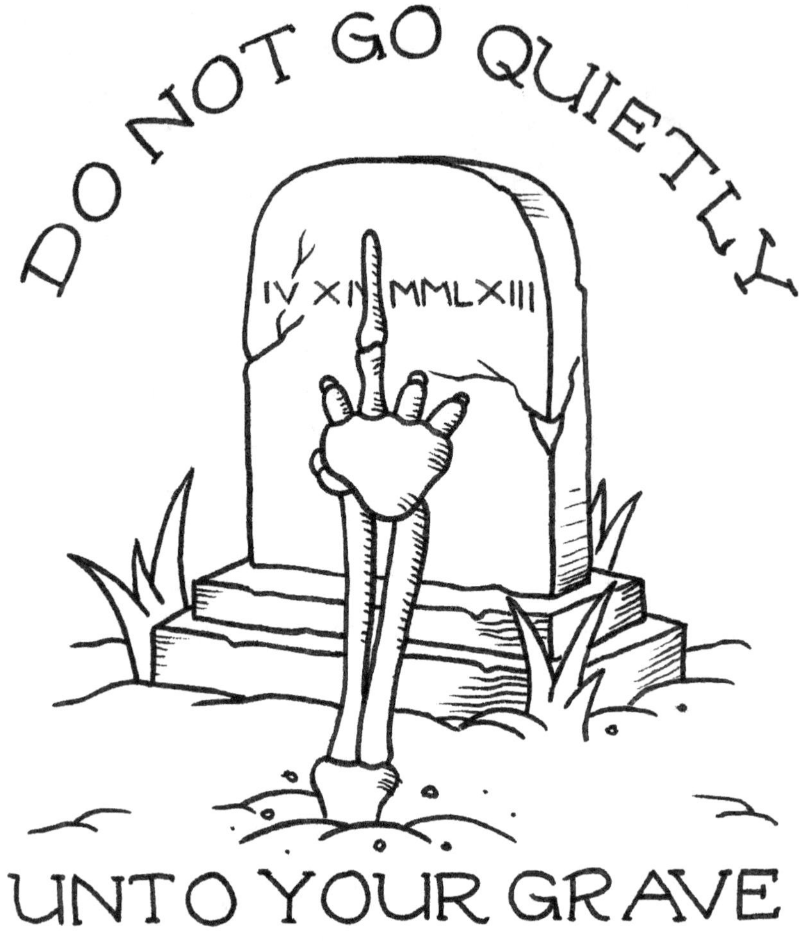

DO NOT GO QUIETLY

IV XIV MMLXIII

UNTO YOUR GRAVE

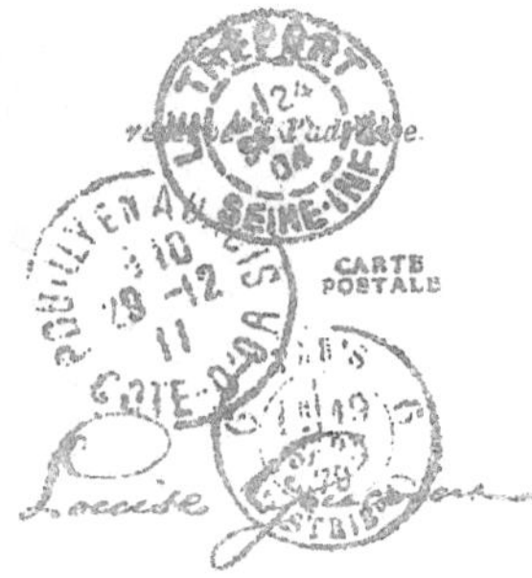

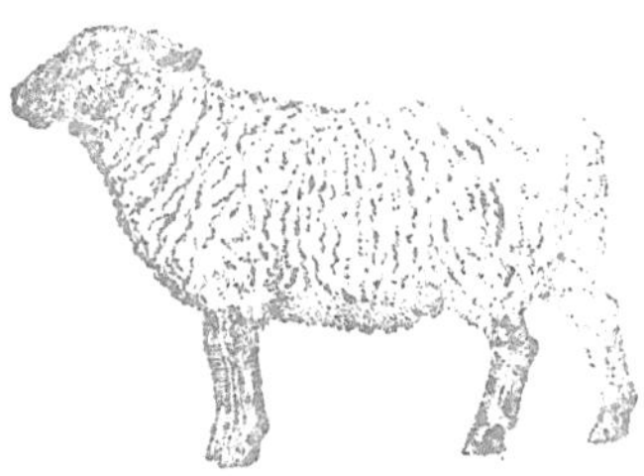

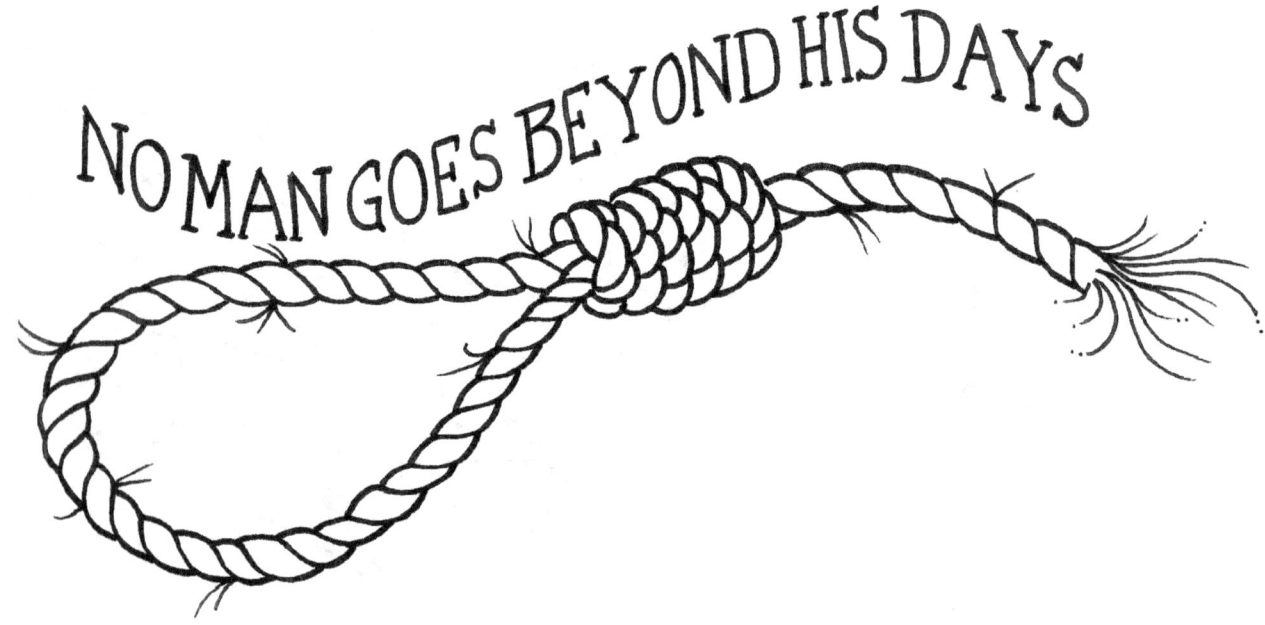

NO MAN GOES BEYOND HIS DAYS

The Pinterest Tattoo Cookbook

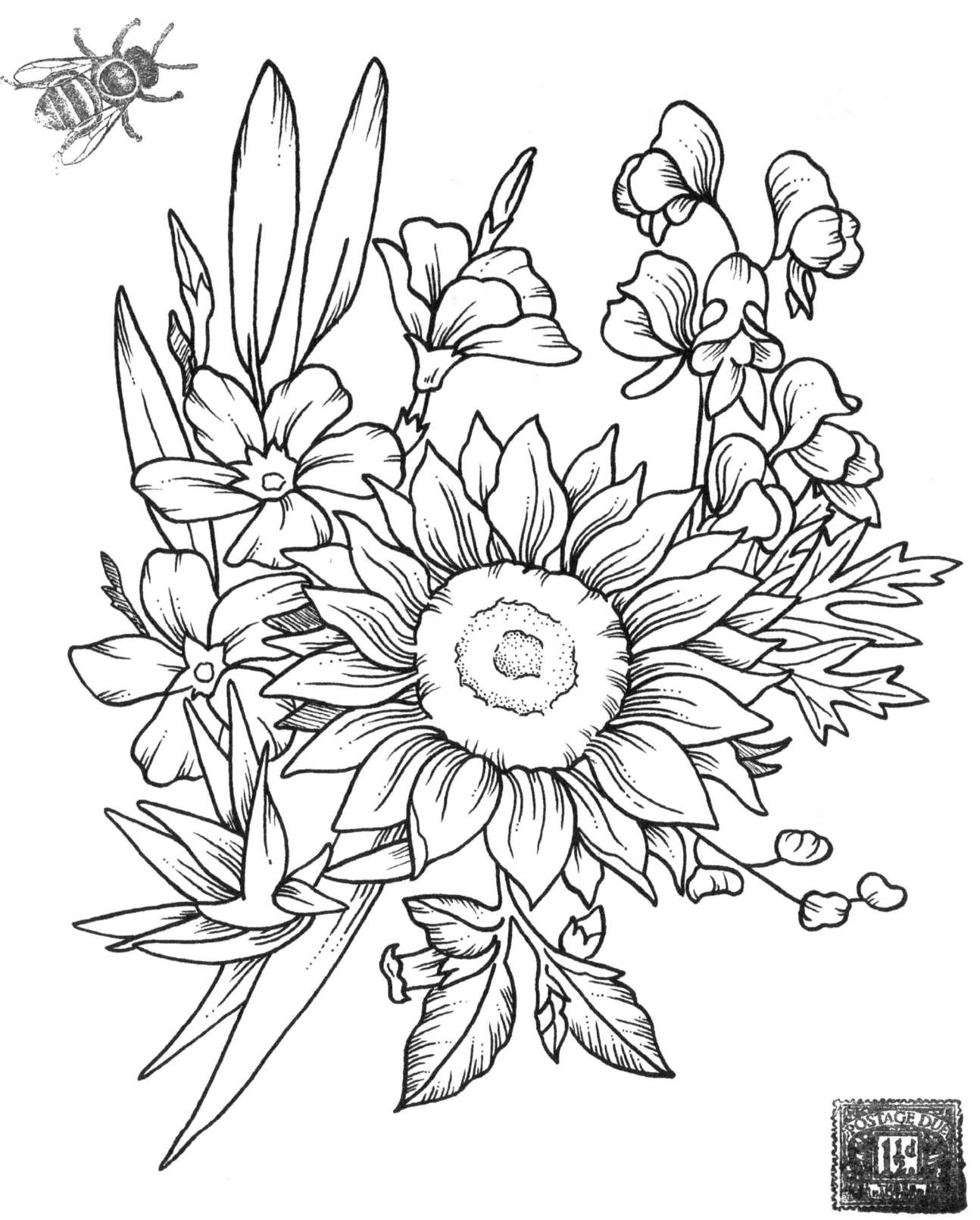

Devin Sheehy

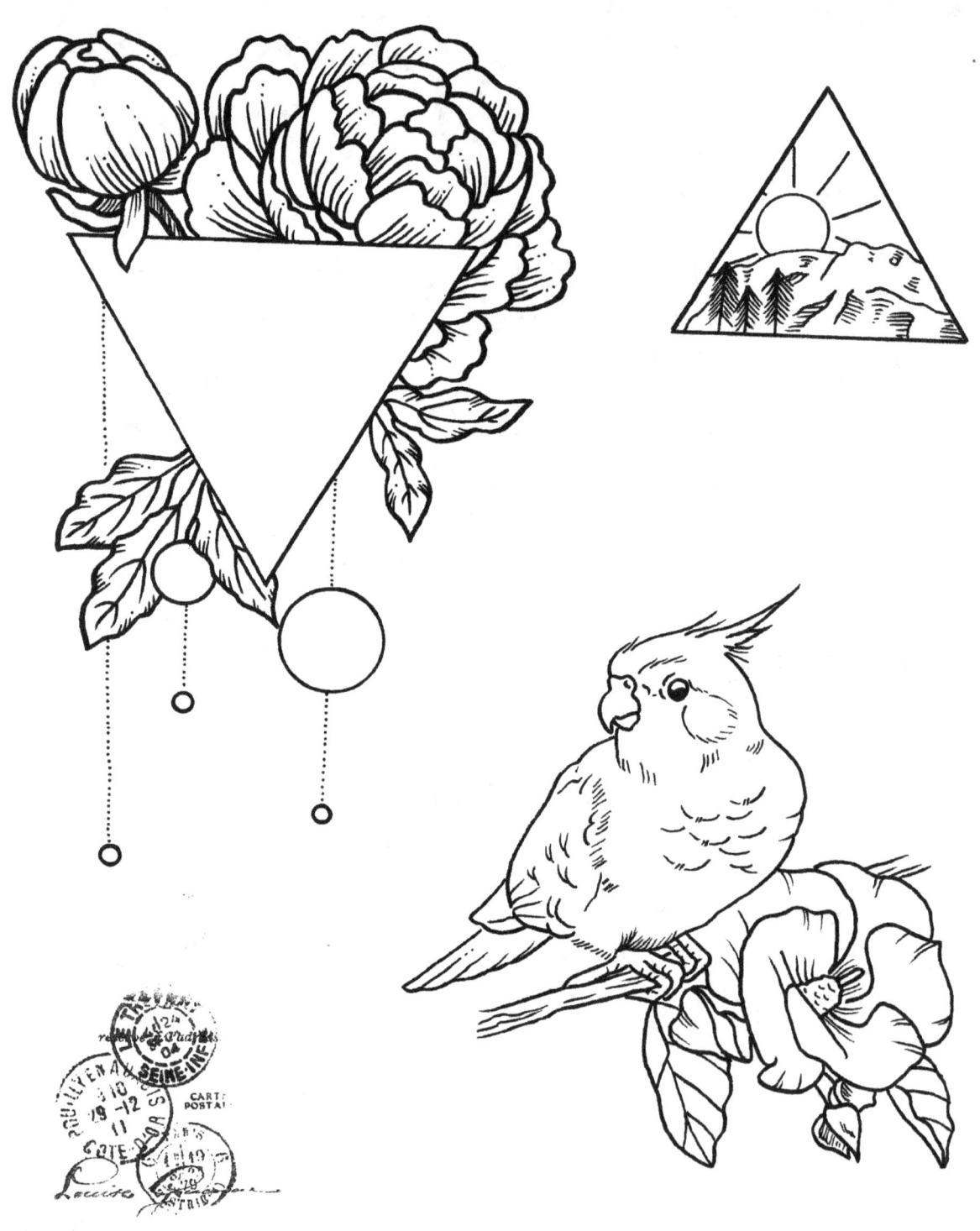

The Pinterest Tattoo Cookbook

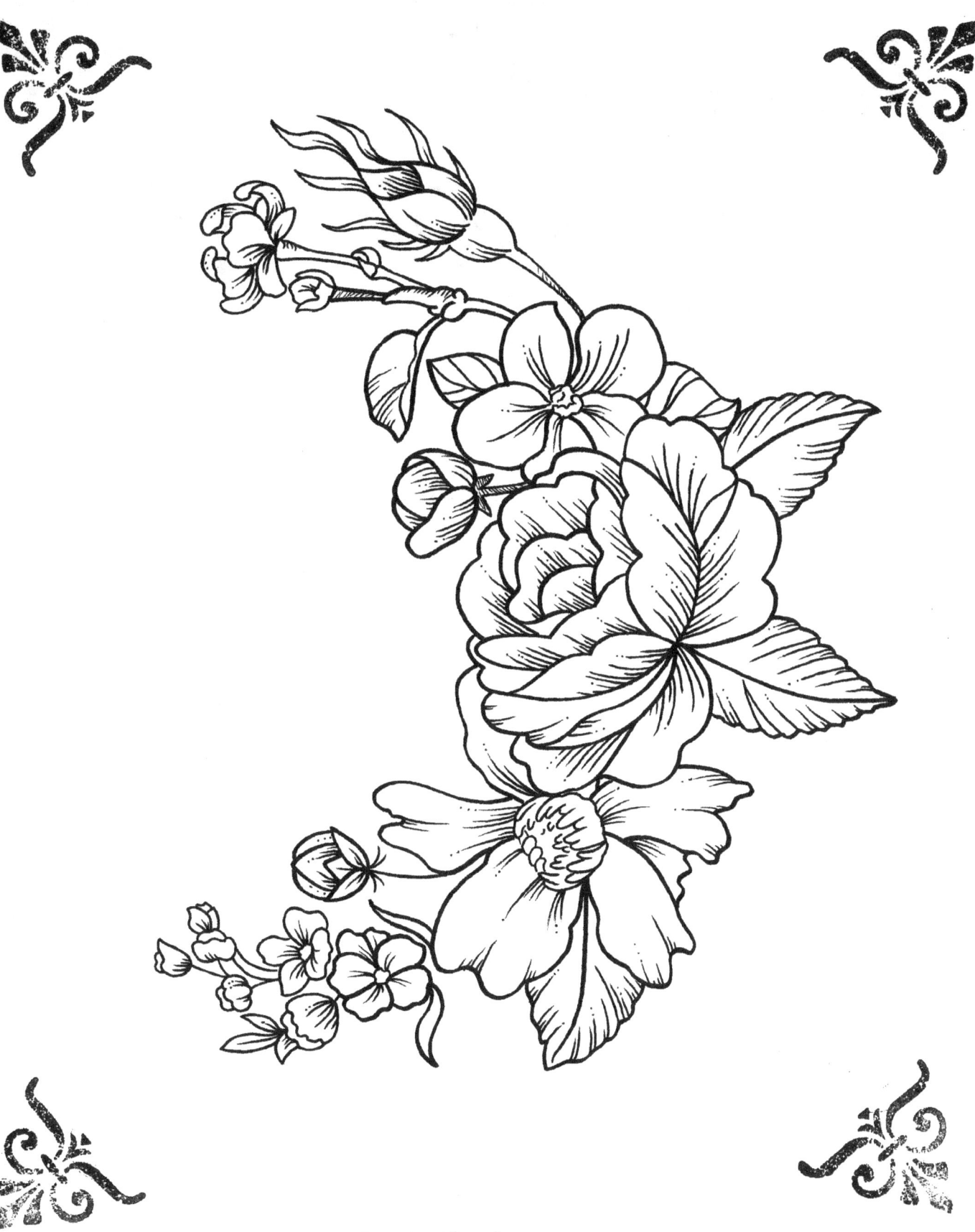

Devin Sheehy

I STILL DANCE

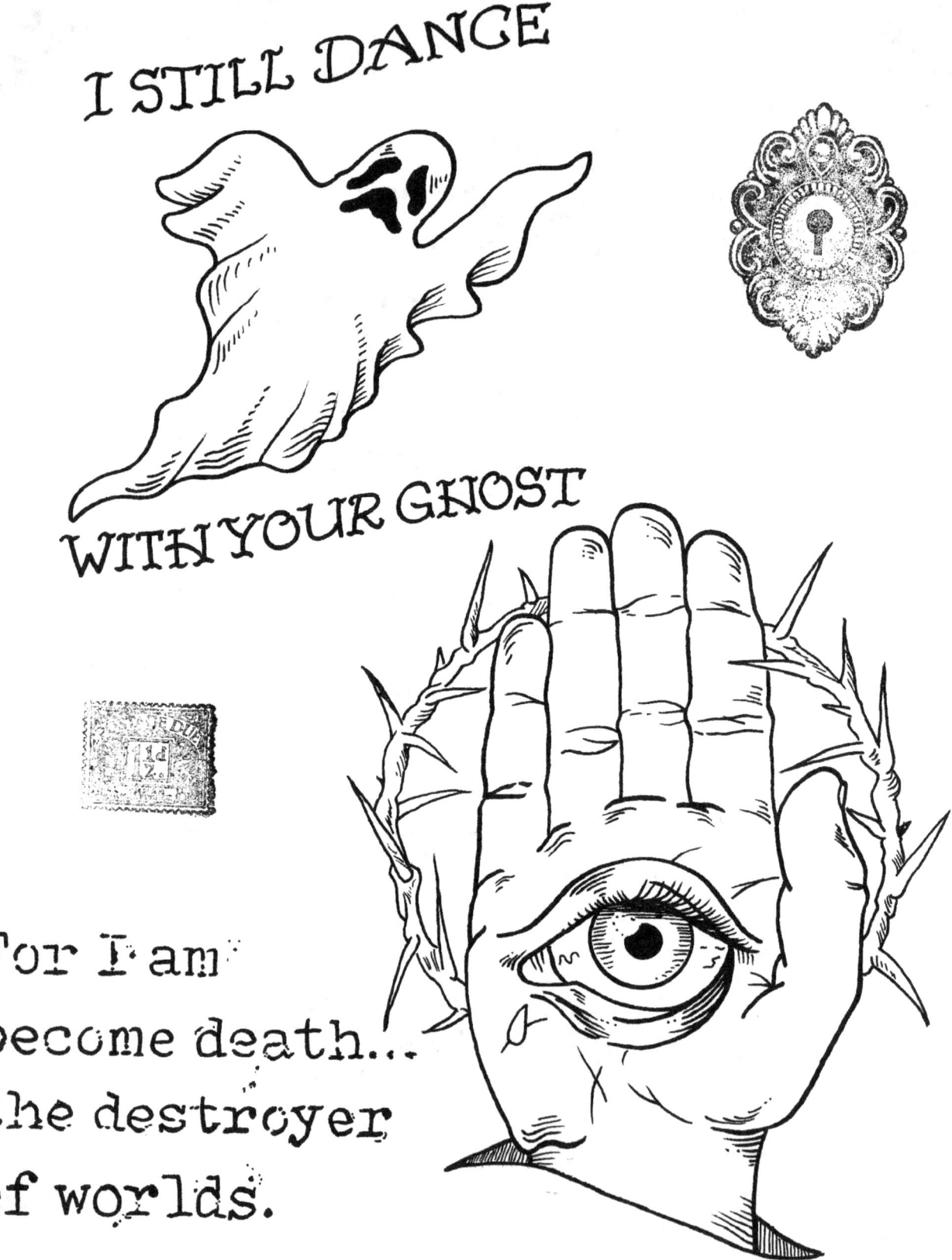

WITH YOUR GHOST

For I am
become death...
the destroyer
of worlds.

The Pinterest Tattoo Cookbook

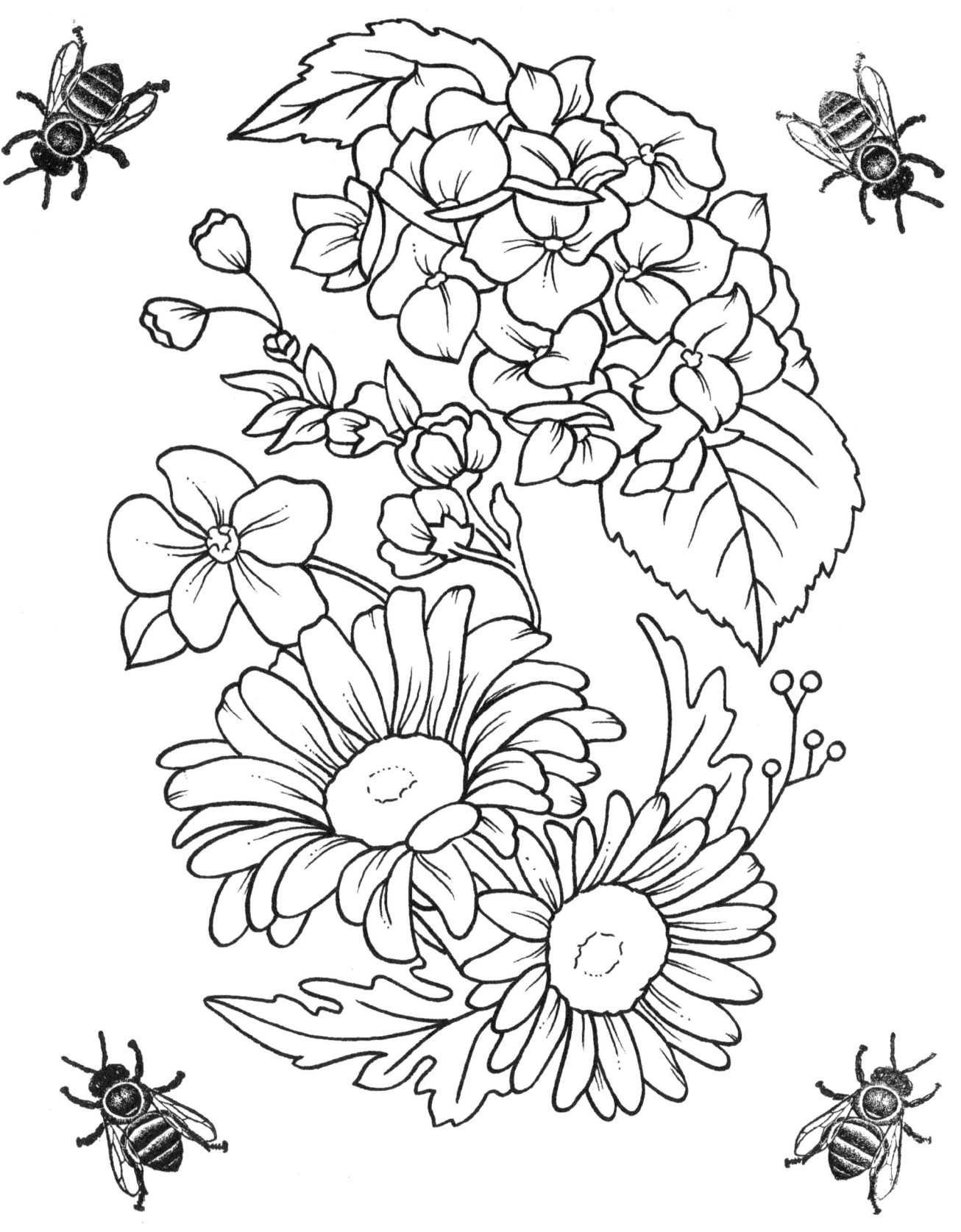

Devin Sheehy

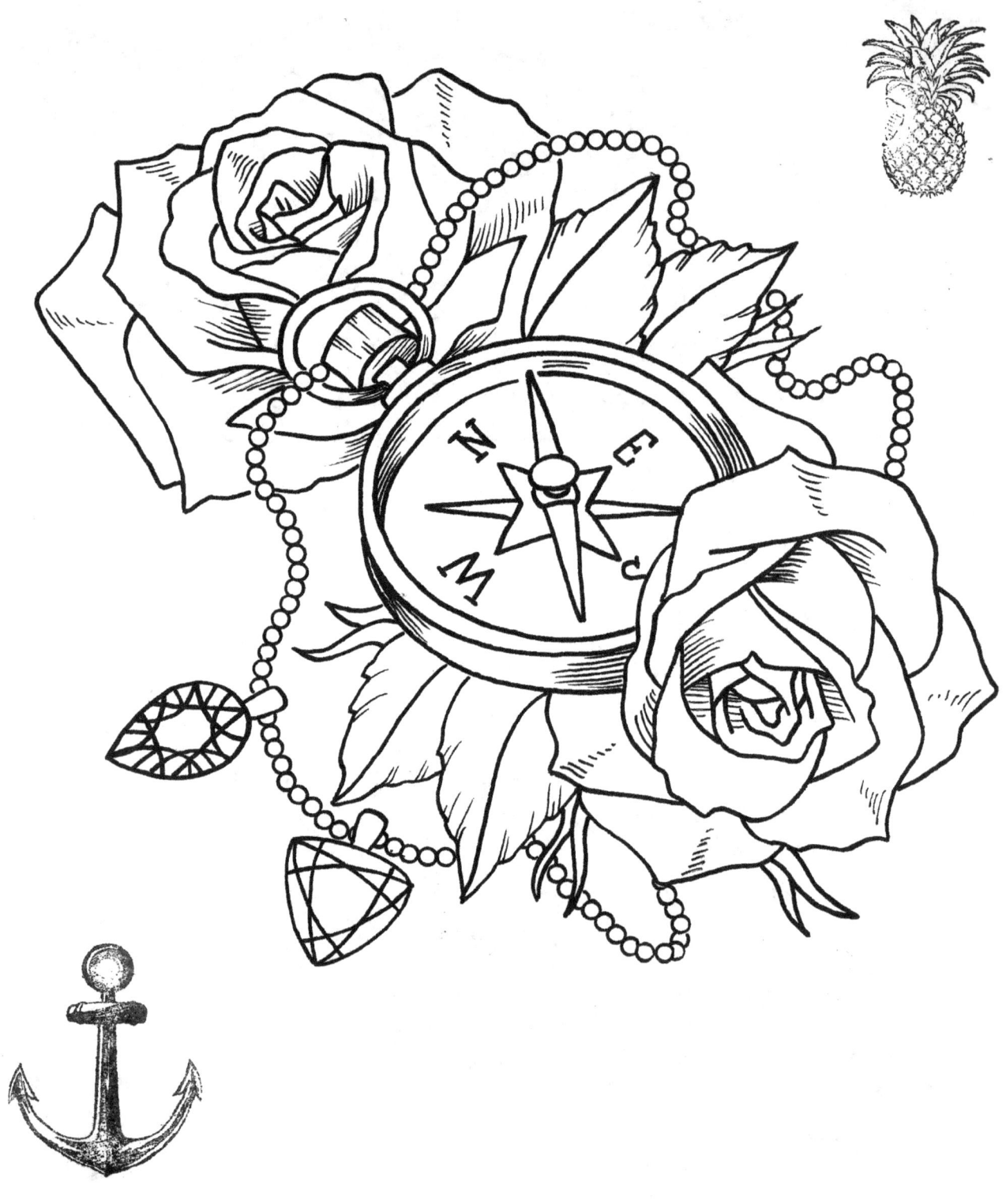

The Pinterest Tattoo Cookbook

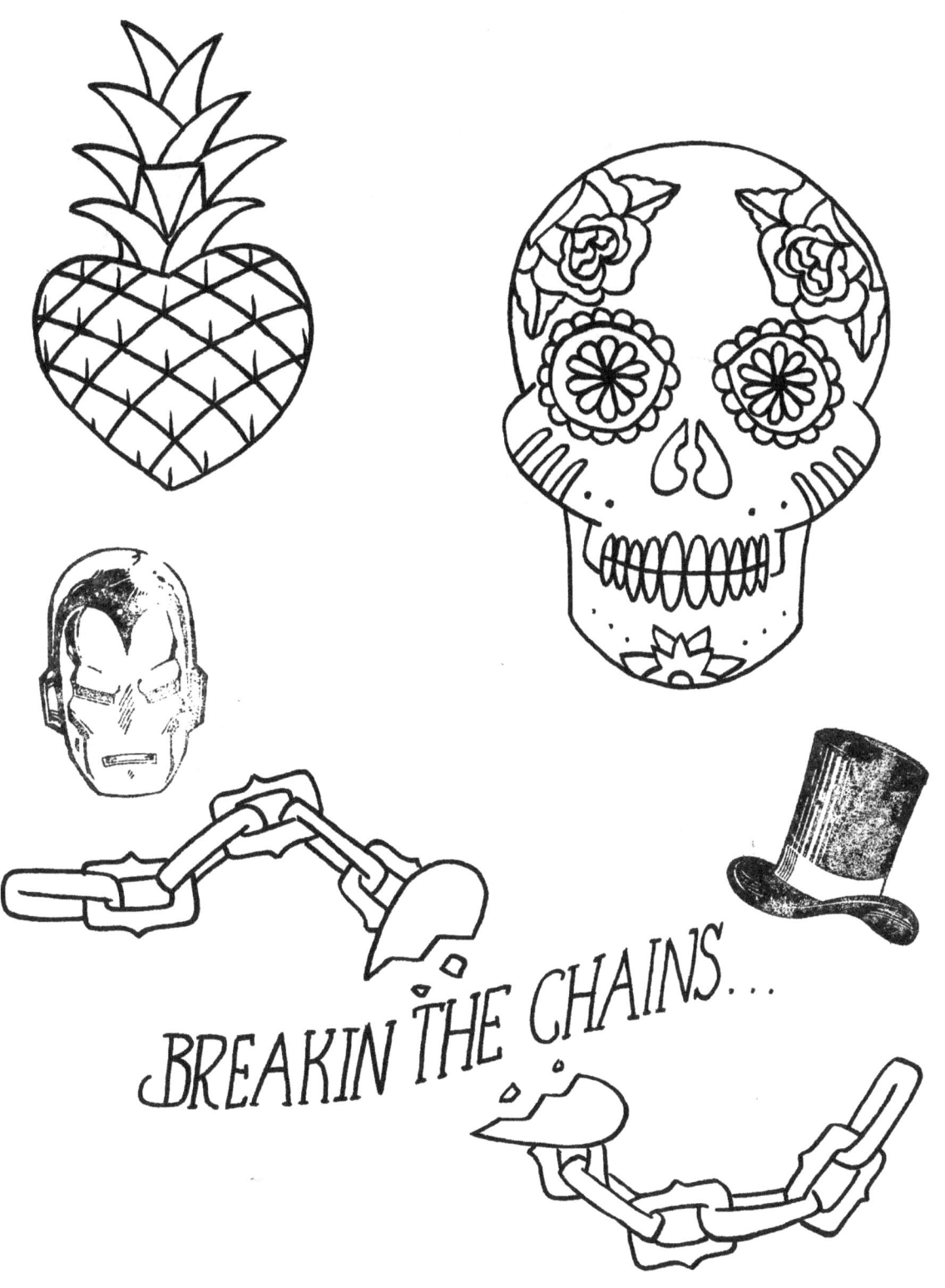

BREAKIN THE CHAINS...

Devin Sheehy

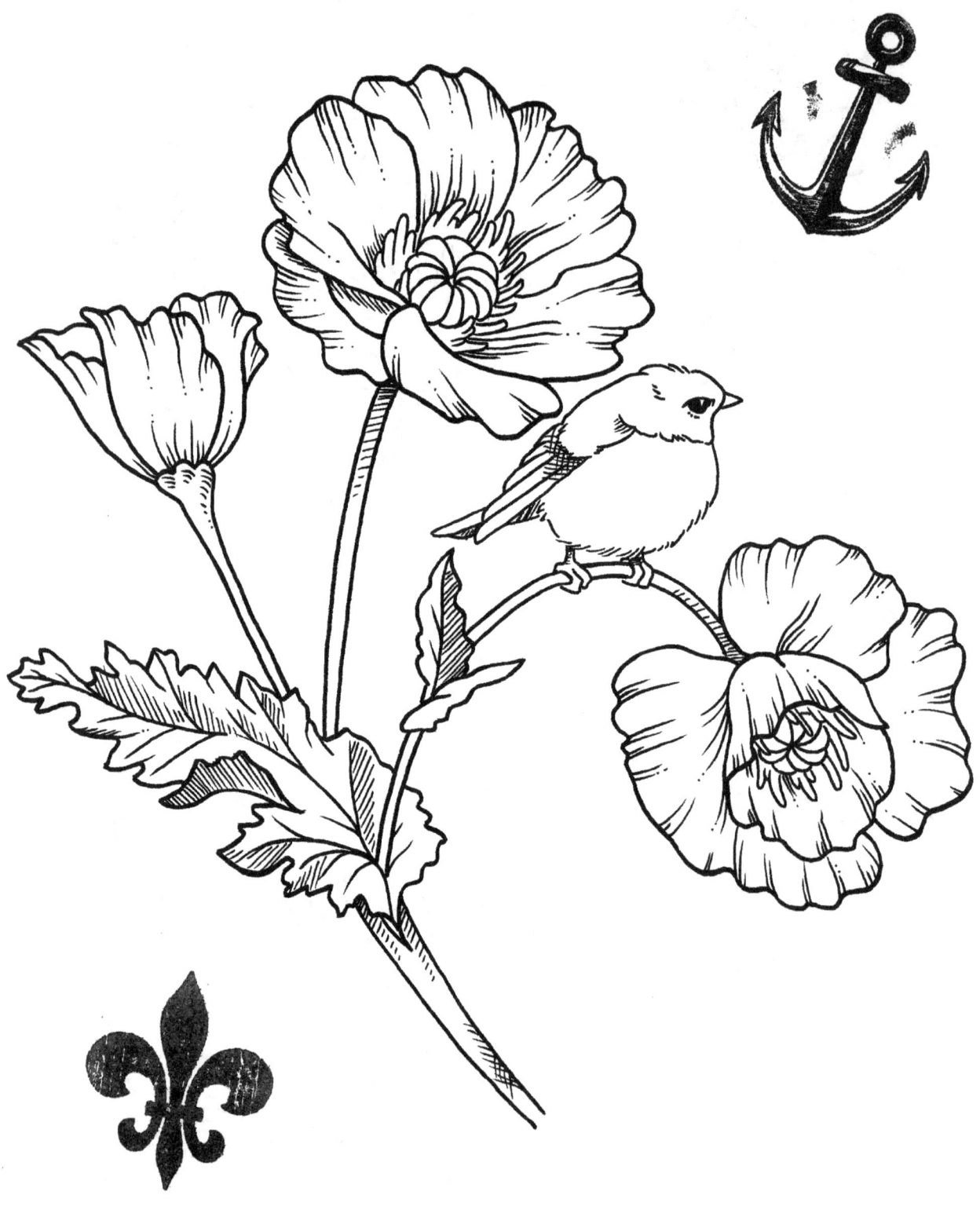

The Pinterest Tattoo Cookbook

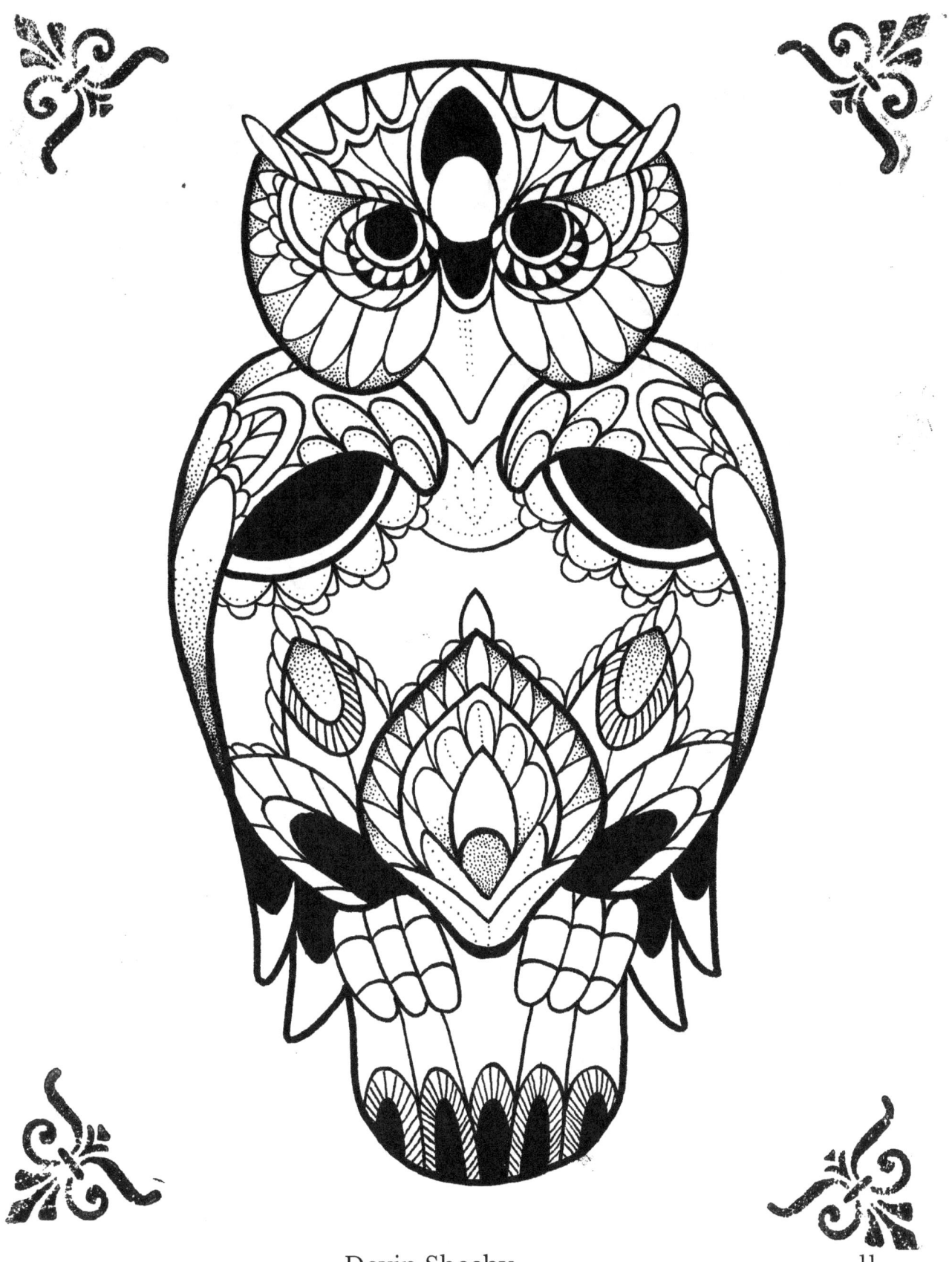

Devin Sheehy

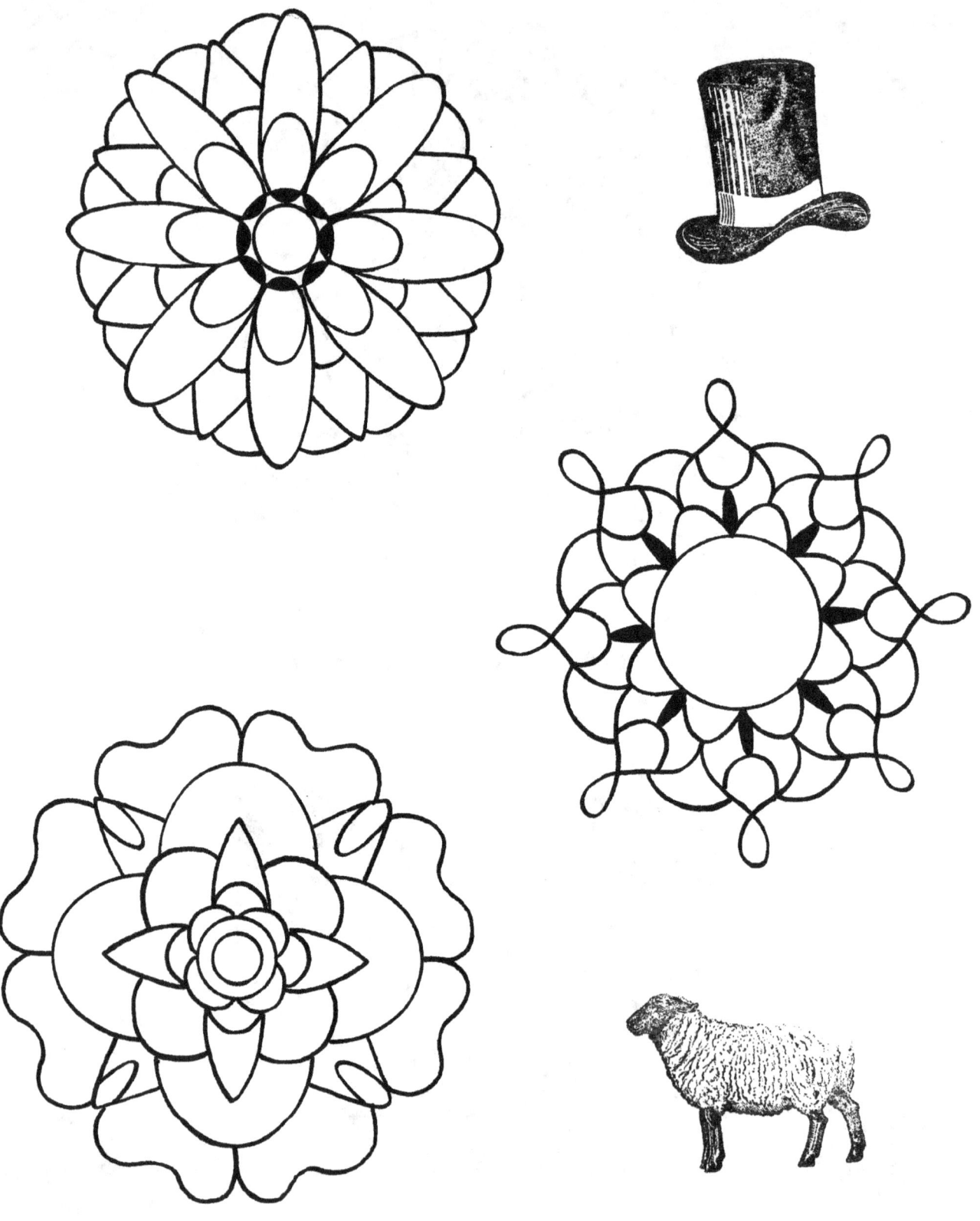

The Pinterest Tattoo Cookbook

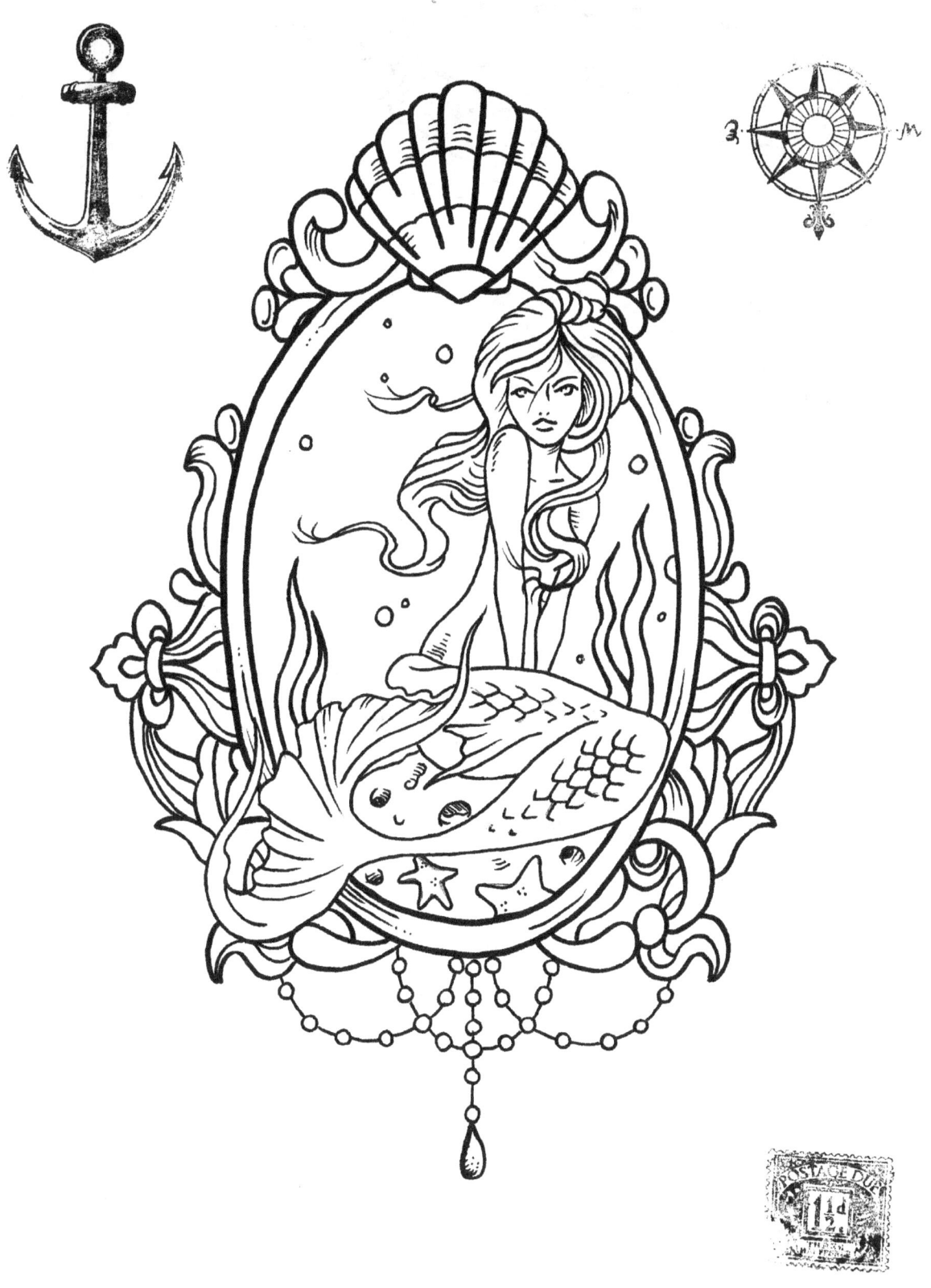

Devin Sheehy   13

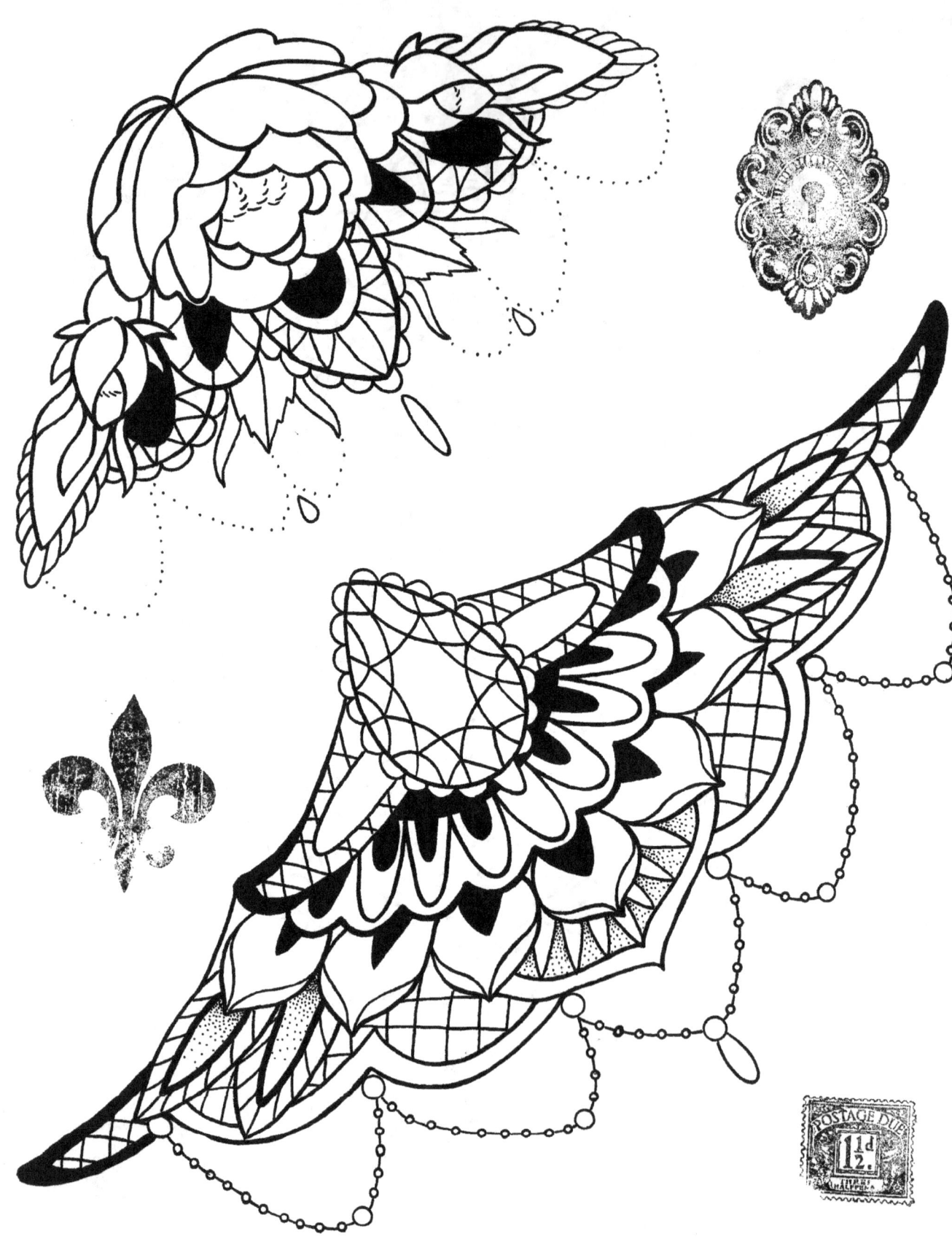

14 The Pinterest Tattoo Cookbook

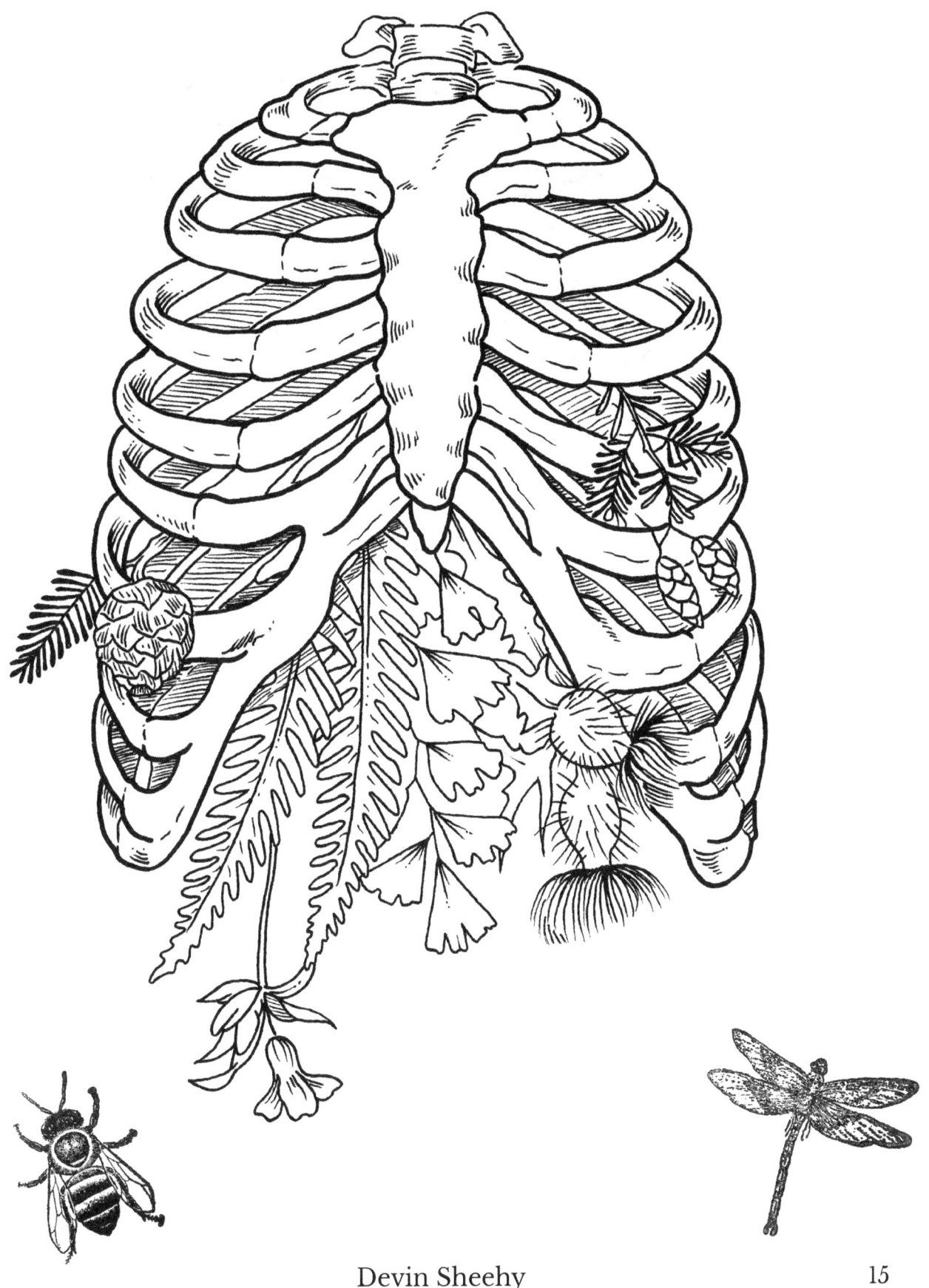

Devin Sheehy

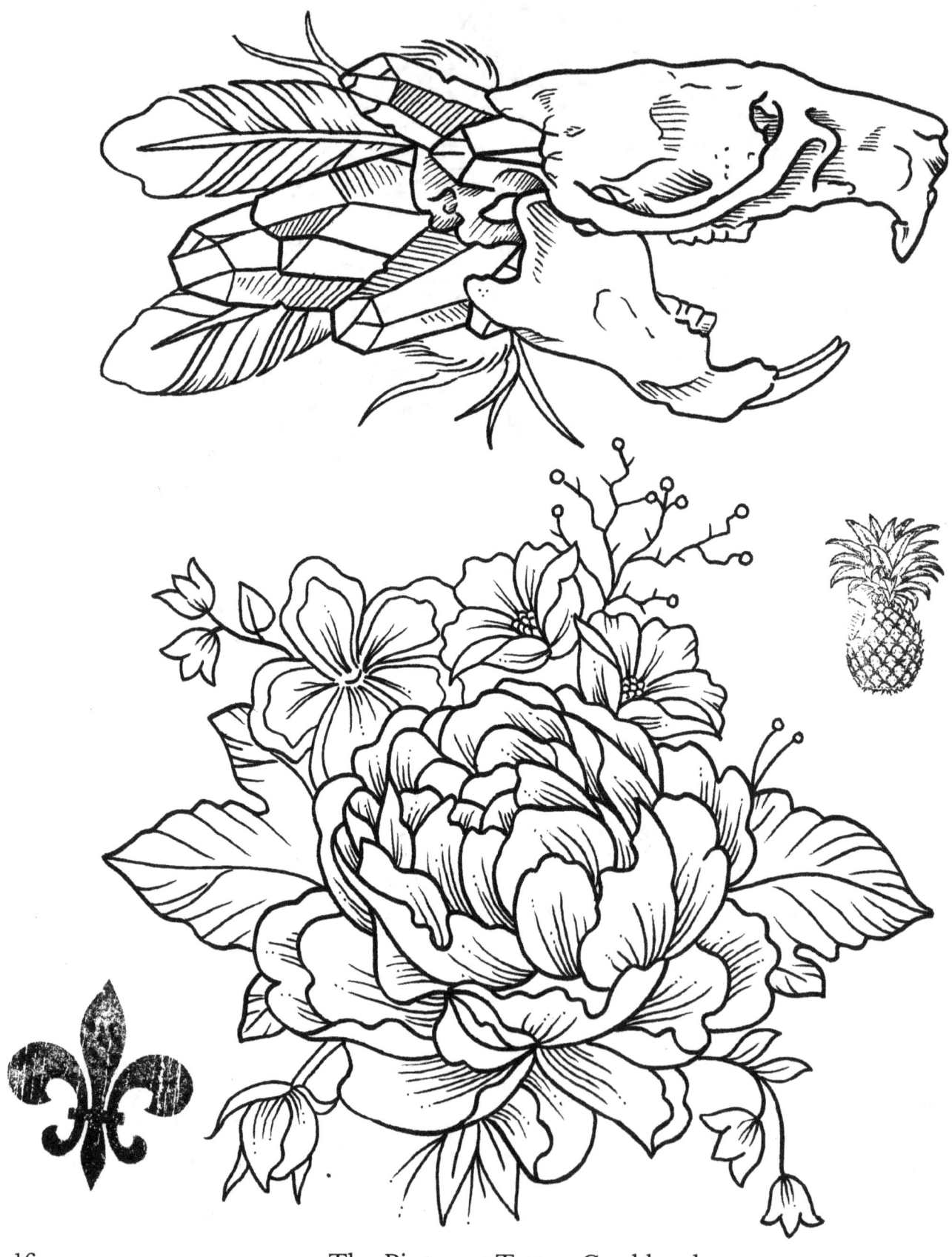

The Pinterest Tattoo Cookbook

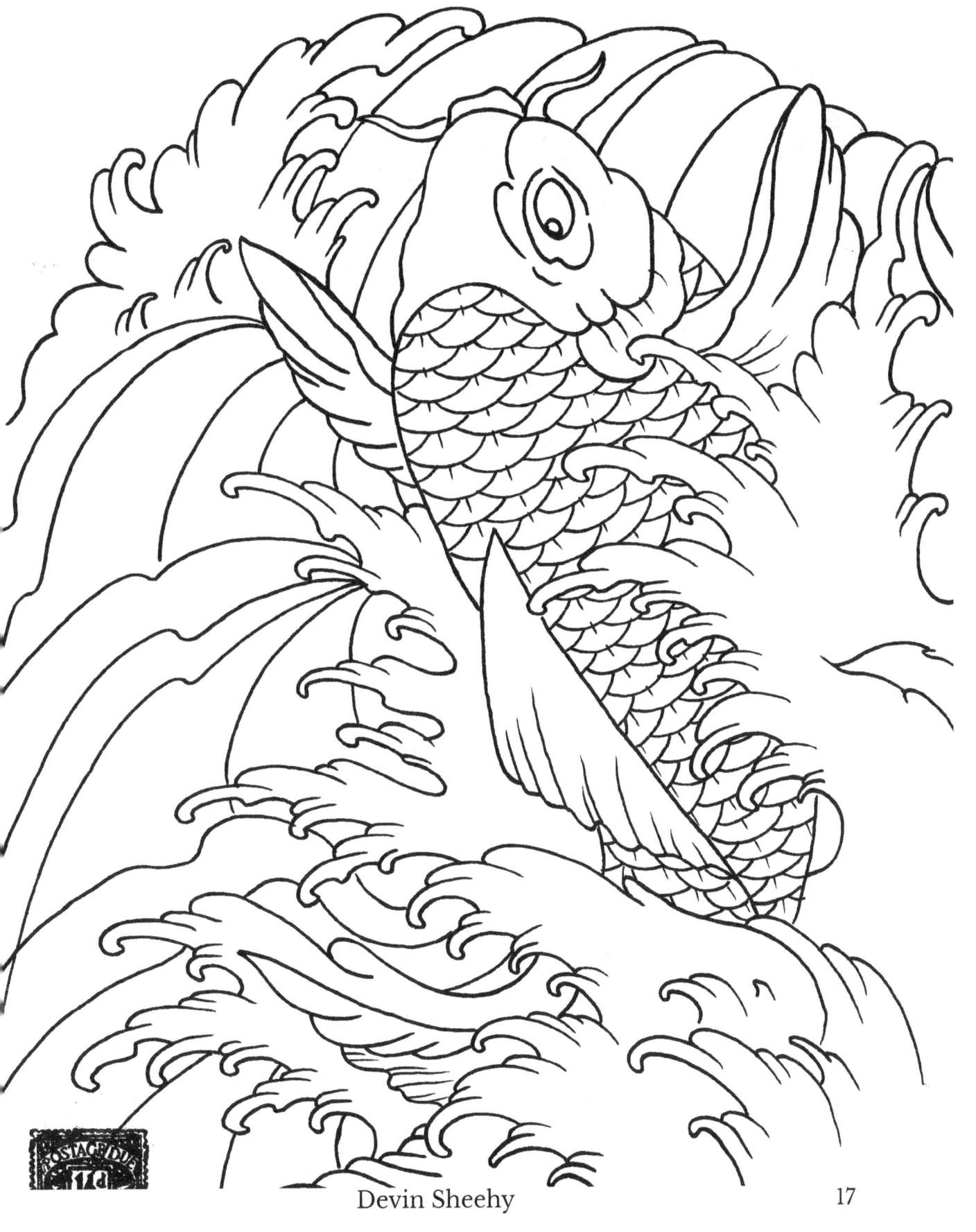

Devin Sheehy

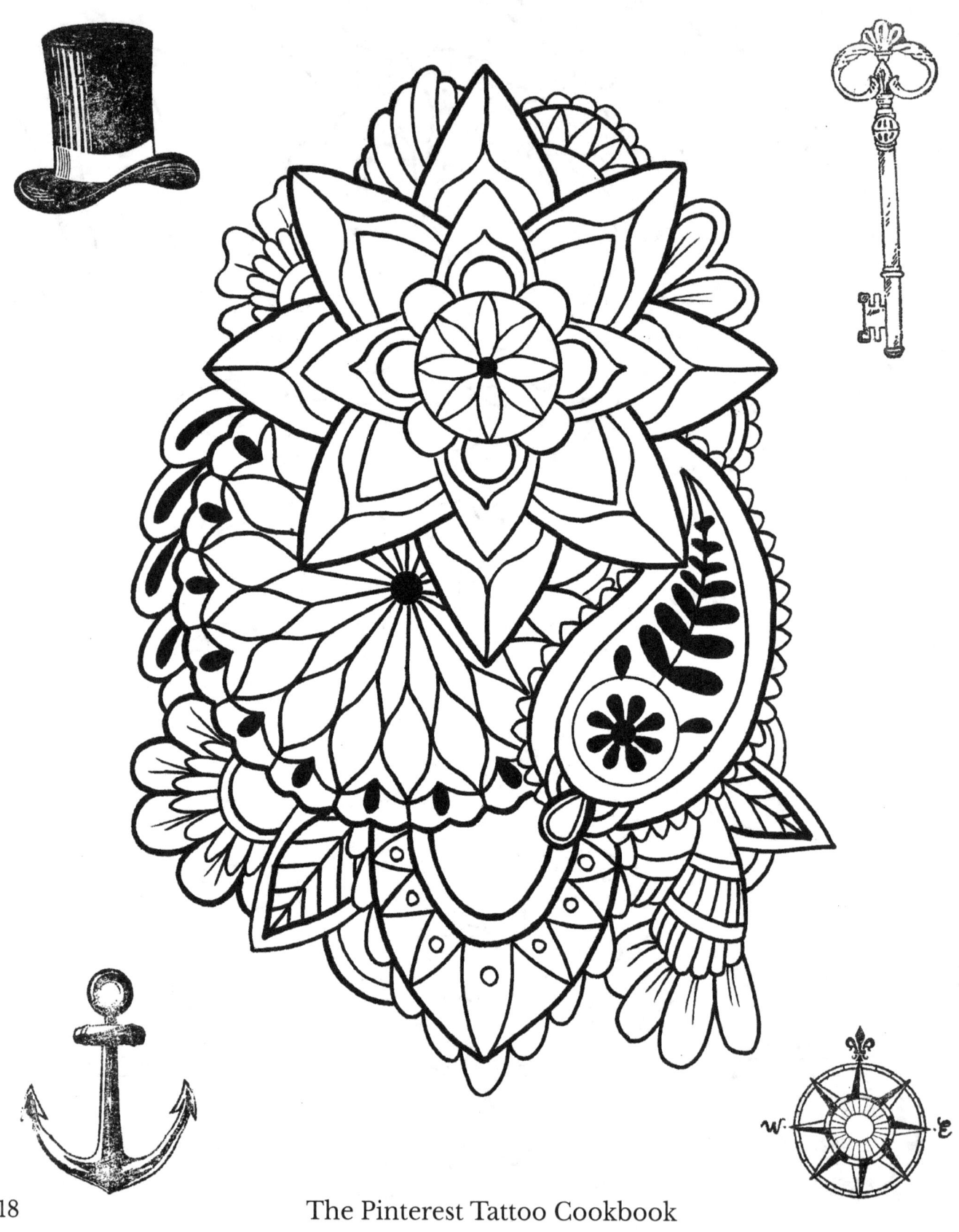

The Pinterest Tattoo Cookbook

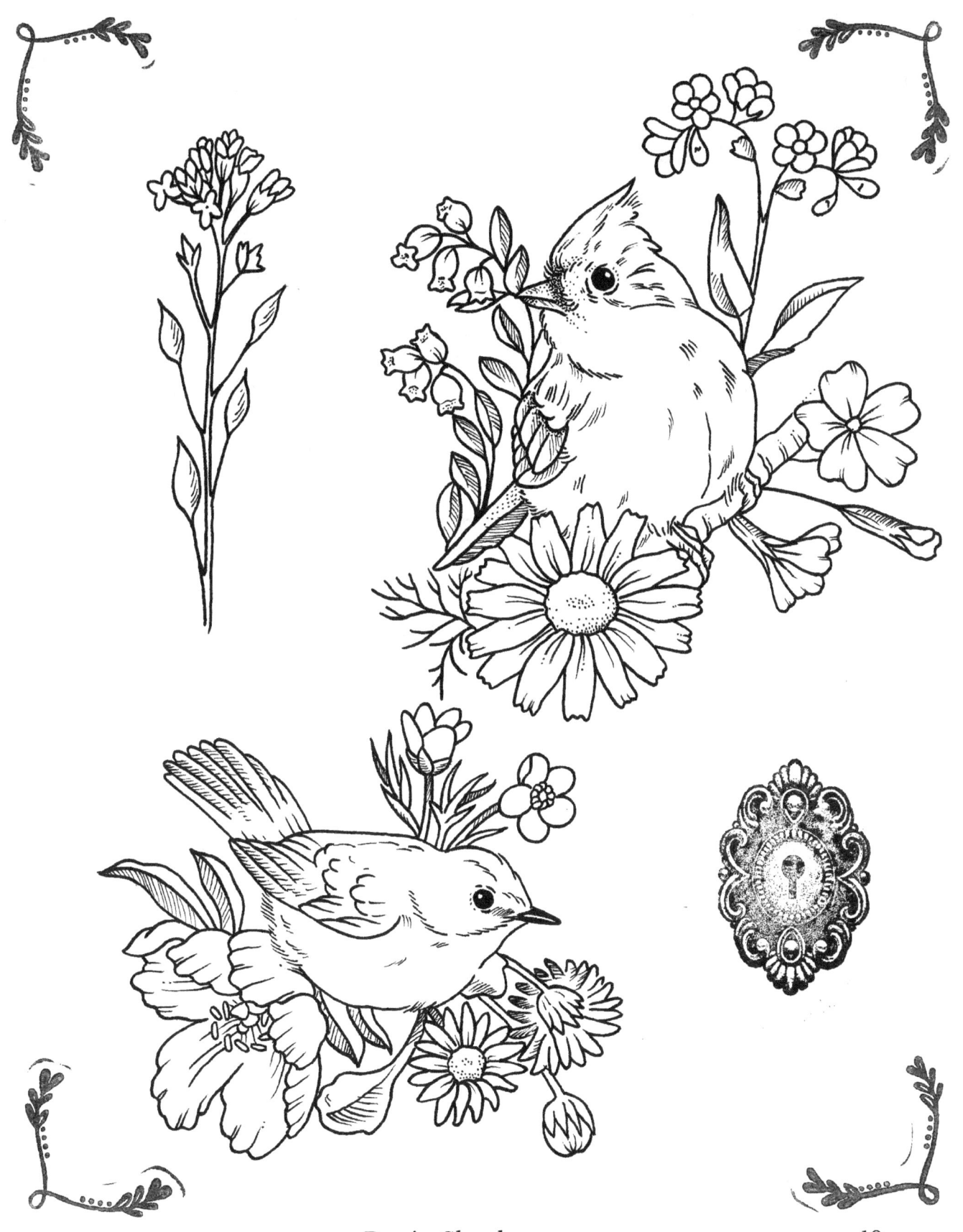

Devin Sheehy

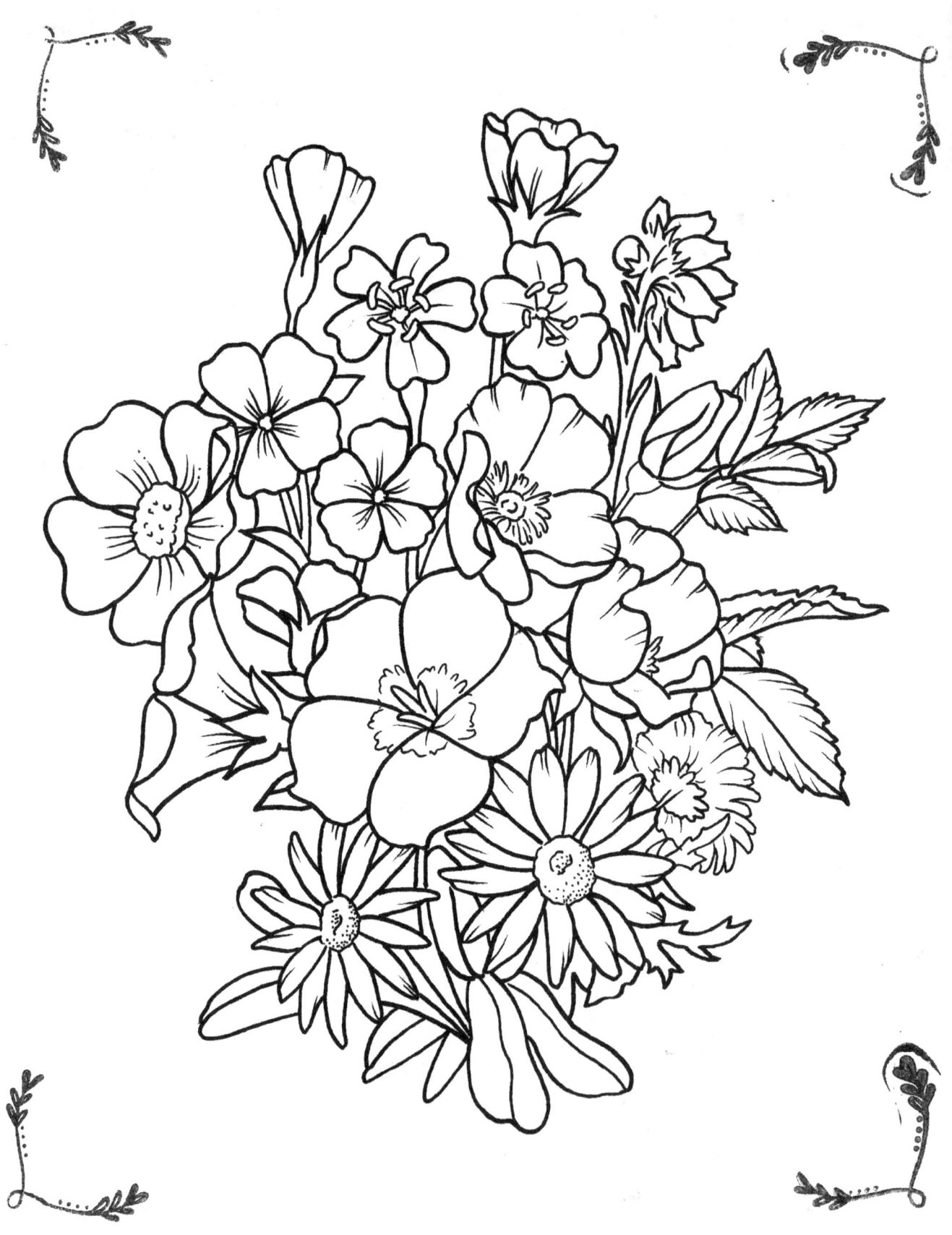

The Pinterest Tattoo Cookbook

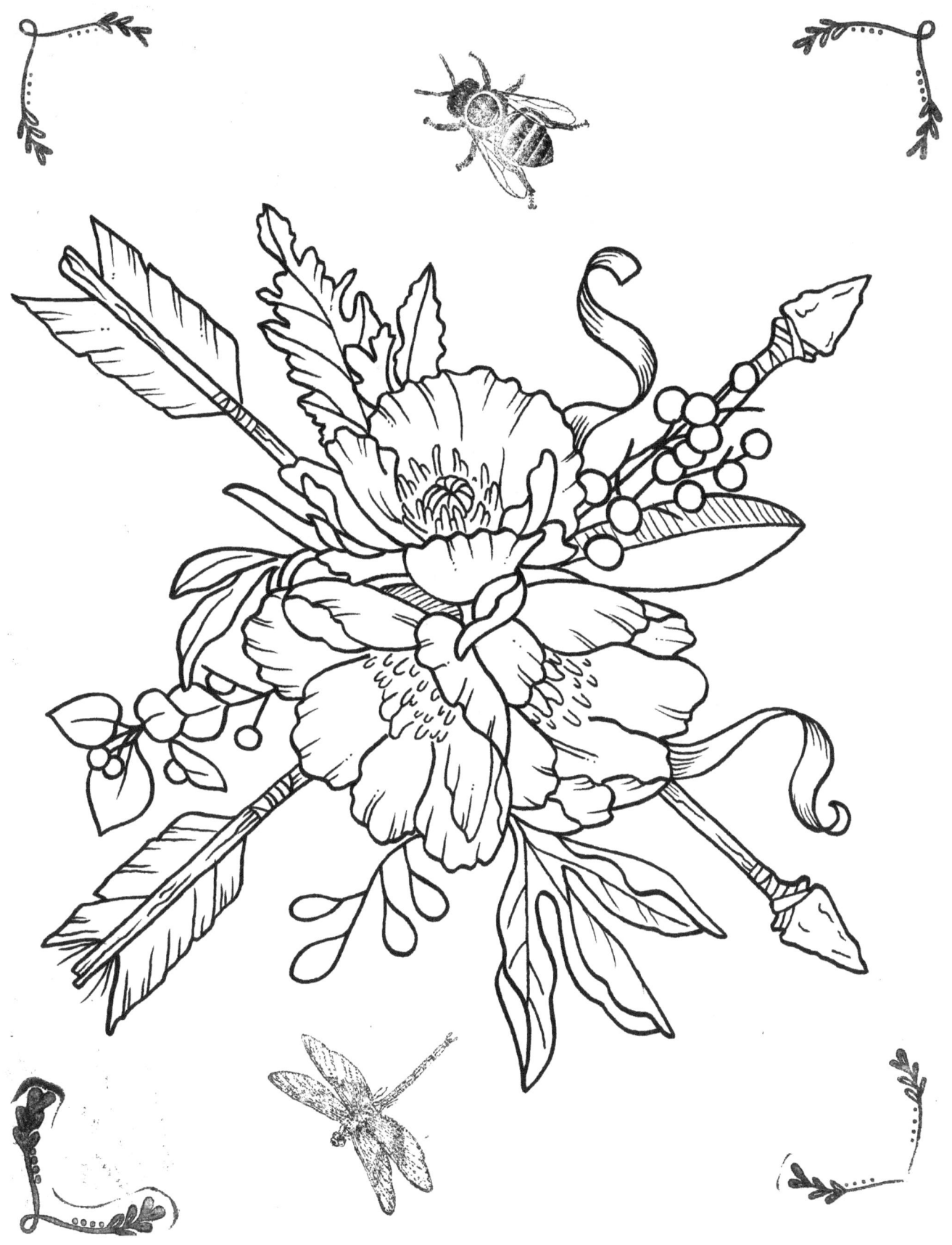

Devin Sheehy

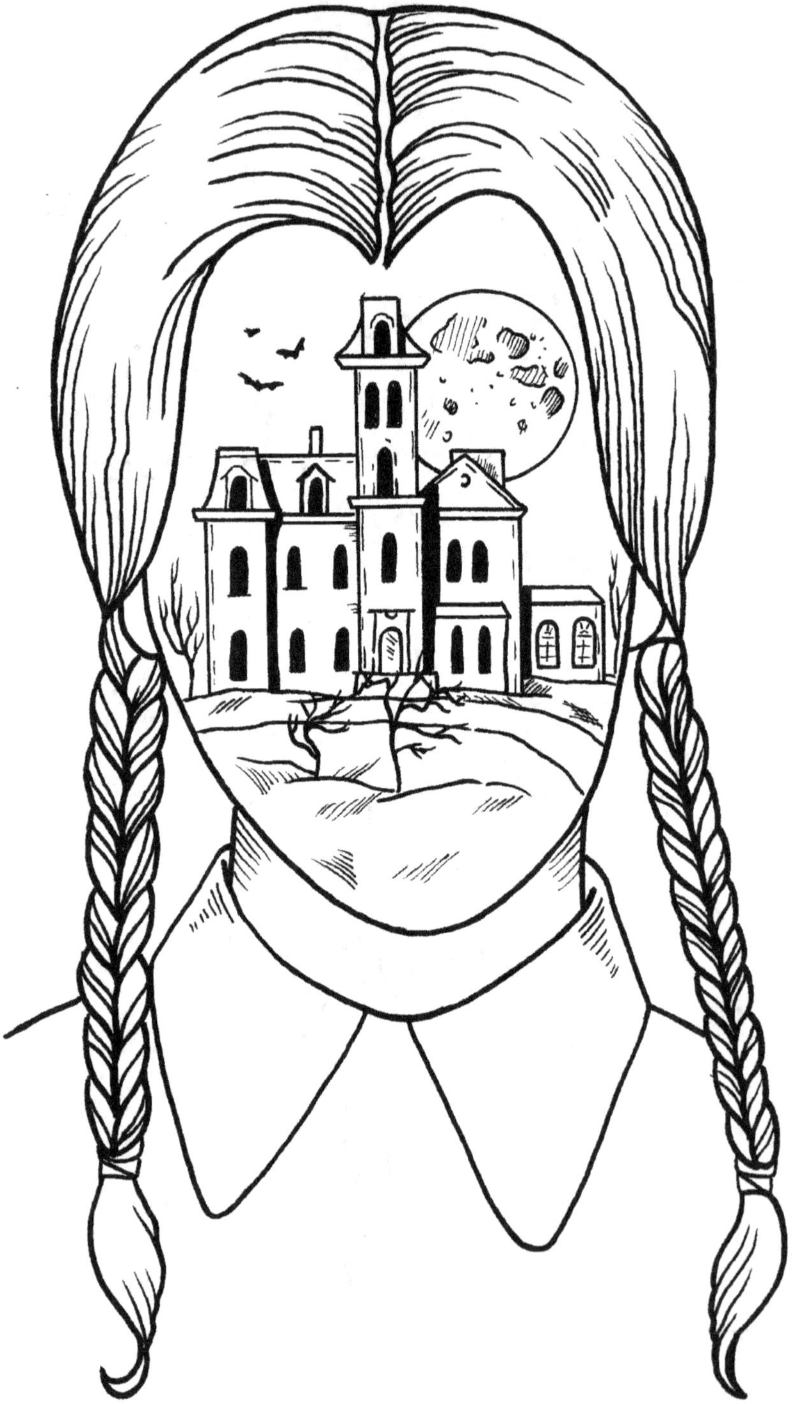

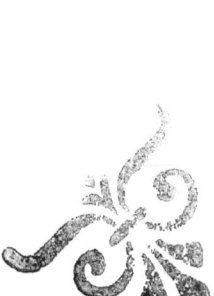

The Pinterest Tattoo Cookbook

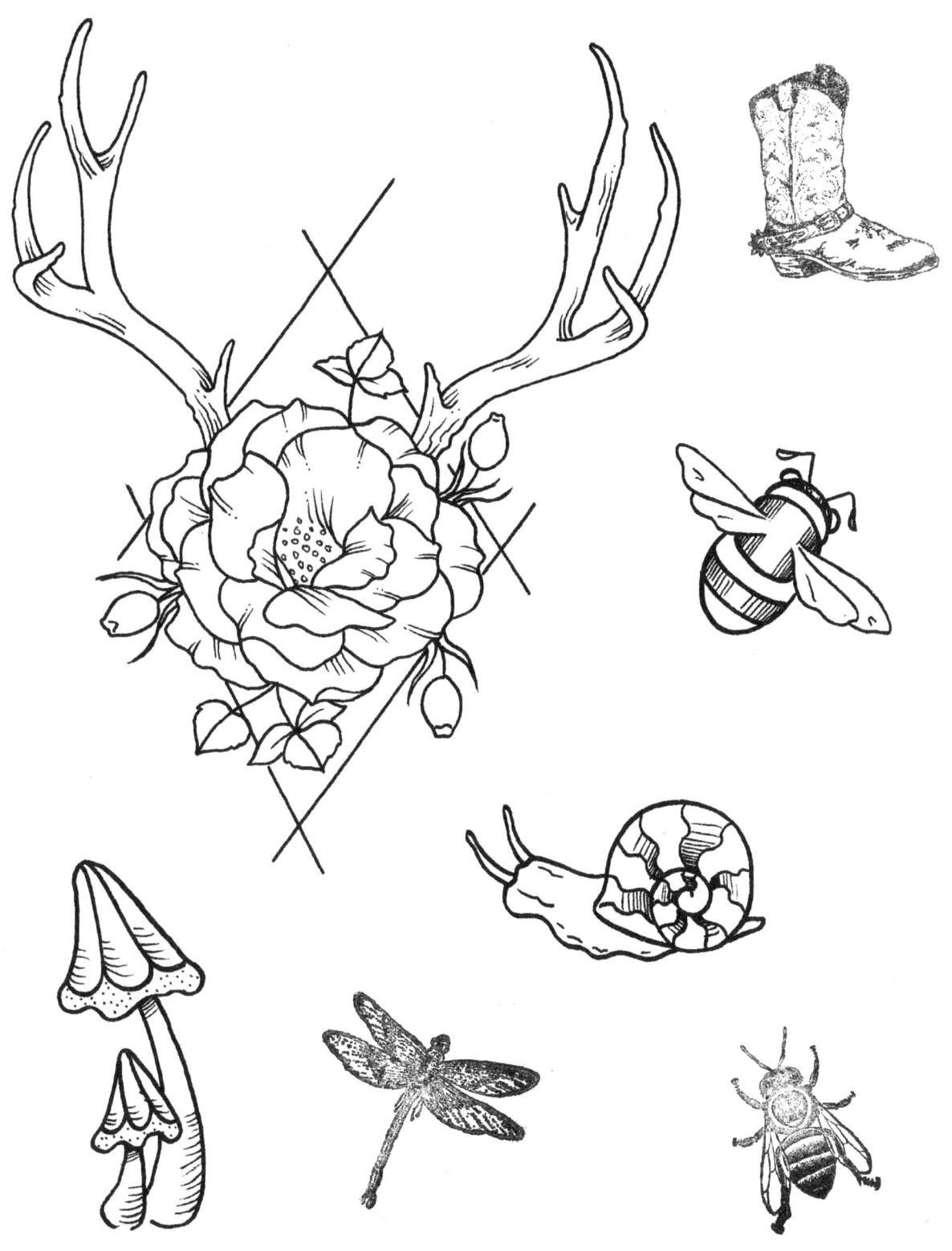

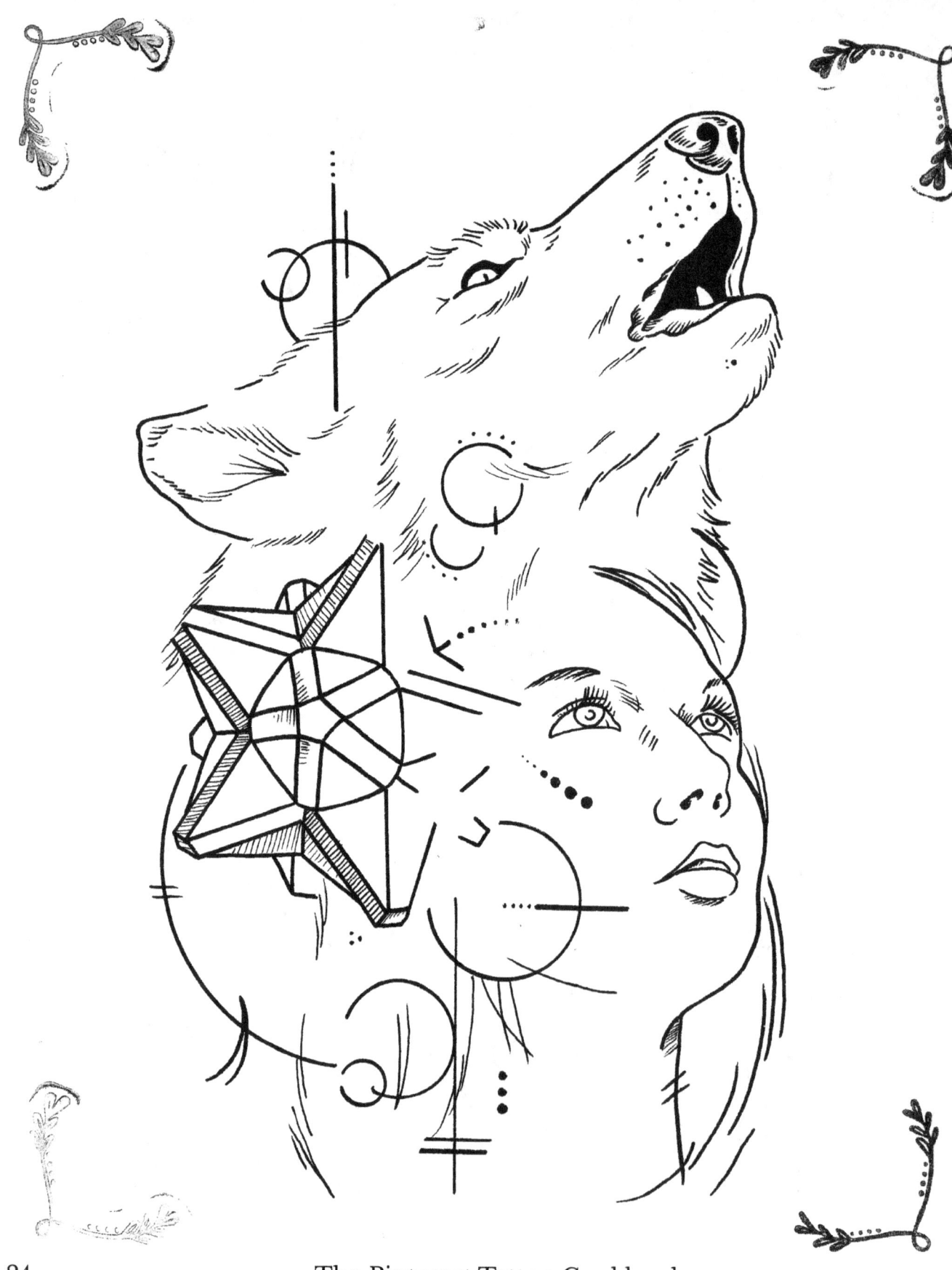

The Pinterest Tattoo Cookbook